JE!
LIF

Bible Reading Plan

Journal # _____

Starting Date: _____

Ending Date: _____

Name: _____

Address: _____

_____ *Phone:* _____

ISBN: 978-0-9992208-1-8

Learn more about becoming a "Jesus freak"
at www.jesusfreakapparel.com

Printed in the United States of America

How the Jesus Freak **LIFE** Journal works

Listen: **"I will teach you and instruct you in the way that you should go…" (Psalms 32:8)**
God is speaking and He wants to walk daily with you! This Life Journal will help you to capture and catalog the lessons He teaches in a way that will help you grow.

Inquire: **"You will seek Me and find Me when you seek Me with all your heart." (Jeremiah 29:13, NIV)**
God wants us to seek Him with all our hearts, and when we do, He meets us right where we're at. This journal will encourage and remind you daily that He waits for you.

Faith: **"Discipline yourself for the purpose of godliness." (1 Timothy 4:7)**
Our faith will grow as we get to know Him more. This journal will help add the substance of faith to your life.

Experience: **"If you know these things, you are blessed if you do them." (John 13:17)**
It is not only knowing things that builds our faith; it is doing them! Applying the lessons God is teaching us brings a blessing.

How to Use the Jesus Freak Life Journal

Step 1:   Use the *Bible Reading Plan* and start on today's date. Check off when complete.

Step 2:   Read the passages. Read with an open heart and Jesus will give you words of encouragement, direction, and correction. (2 Timothy 3:16)

Step 3:   When Jesus gives you a life lesson, turn to a journal page and record what He has shown you. SOAP method of Scripture:
- Write in today's date.
- Give your lesson a title.
- Write down your main Scripture. (**S**cripture)
- Write what you see in Scripture. (**O**bservation)
- Write how you will be different today because of what you have just read. (**A**pplication)
- Write out your prayer. (**P**rayer)
  (See example on page)

Step 4:   Conclude your daily devotional time by praying for what you have written.

Remember: The *Jesus Freak Life Journal* is designed to serve you in your growth with Christ. You can be flexible in how you use it, but be sure to develop a healthy habit of spending time daily with the Lord.

Some have asked, "When is the best time for my devotions? In the morning or in the evening?"

My answer to that is, "The best time is when you're at your best!" If you're a morning person, do your devotions in the morning. If you're an evening person do your devotions at night. The bottom line is: "Jesus deserves your best, so give Him the best part of your day!"

Jesus Freak Life Journal Sample Entry

Date   **Title**
4/23   Marching Orders

Scripture: "What I tell you in the darkness, speak in the
light; and what you hear whispered in your ear,
proclaim upon the housetops." Matthew 10:27

Observation: If I am not hearing Him in the darkness, what
will I speak in the light? If I am not hearing
Him whisper in my ear, what will I proclaim
on the housetops?

Application: What a great word! This scripture reminds me
to not only talk to God in prayer, but equally
important is to hear Him in prayer.

Prayer: "Dear Jesus, help me to hear You today! I want
to be still that I may hear Your marching orders
for my day, for my week, for my life. Speak
Lord. Your servant is listening."

Jesus Freak Life Journal
Bible Reading Plan
Your personal reading schedule to take you
through the entire Bible within a year.

January

1 ◯ Genesis 1,2; Luke 1
2 ◯ Genesis 3-5; Luke 2
3 ◯ Genesis 6-8; Luke 3
4 ◯ Genesis 9-11; Luke 4
5 ◯ Genesis 12-14; Luke 5
6 ◯ Genesis 15-17; Luke 6
7 ◯ Genesis 18,19; Ps. 3; Luke 7
8 ◯ Genesis 20-22; Luke 8
9 ◯ Genesis 23,24; Luke 9
10 ◯ Genesis 25,26; Ps. 6; Luke 10
11 ◯ Gen. 27,28; Ps. 4; Luke 11
12 ◯ Genesis 29,30; Luke 12
13 ◯ Genesis 31-33; Luke 13
14 ◯ Genesis 34-36; Luke 14
15 ◯ Gen. 37,38; Ps. 7; Luke 15
16 ◯ Genesis 39-41; Luke 16
17 ◯ Gen. 42,43; Ps. 5; Luke 17
18 ◯ Genesis 44-46; Luke 18
19 ◯ Gen. 47,48; Ps. 10; Luke 19
20 ◯ Gen. 49,50; Ps. 8; Luke 20
21 ◯ Exodus 1,2; Ps. 88; Luke 21
22 ◯ Exodus 3-5; Luke 22
23 ◯ Exodus 6-8; Luke 23
24 ◯ Exodus 9-11; Luke 24
25 ◯ Exodus 12,13; Ps. 21; Acts 1
26 ◯ Exodus 14-16; Acts 2
27 ◯ Exodus 17-20; Acts 3
28 ◯ Exodus 21,22; Ps. 12; Acts 4
29 ◯ Exodus 23,24; Ps. 14; Acts 5
30 ◯ Exodus 25-27; Acts 6
31 ◯ Exodus 28,29; Acts 7

February

1 ◯ Exodus 30-32; Acts 8
2 ◯ Exodus 33,34; Ps. 16; Acts 9
3 ◯ Exodus 35,36; Acts 10
4 ◯ Exodus 37,38; Ps. 19; Acts 11
5 ◯ Exodus 39,40; Ps. 15; Acts 12
6 ◯ Leviticus 1-3; Acts 13
7 ◯ Leviticus 4-6; Acts 14
8 ◯ Leviticus 7-9; Acts 15
9 ◯ Leviticus 10-12; Acts 16
10 ◯ Leviticus 13,14; Acts 17
11 ◯ Leviticus 15-17; Acts 18
12 ◯ Leviticus 18,19; Ps. 13; Acts 19
13 ◯ Leviticus 20-22; Acts 20
14 ◯ Leviticus 23,24; Ps. 24; Acts 21
15 ◯ Leviticus 25; Ps. 25,26; Acts 22
16 ◯ Leviticus 26,27; Acts 23
17 ◯ Numbers 1,2; Acts 24
18 ◯ Numbers 3,4; Acts 25
19 ◯ Numbers 5,6; Ps. 22; Acts 26
20 ◯ Numbers 7; Ps. 23; Acts 27
21 ◯ Numbers 8,9; Acts 28
22 ◯ Numbers 10,11; Ps. 27; Mark 1
23 ◯ Numbers 12,13; Ps. 90; Mark 2
24 ◯ Numbers 14-16; Mark 3
25 ◯ Numbers 17,18; Ps. 29; Mark 4
26 ◯ Numbers 19,20; Ps. 28; Mark 5
27 ◯ Numbers 21-23; Mark 6,7
28 ◯ Numbers 24-27; 1 Corinthians 13

March

1 ◯ Numbers 28,29; Mark 8
2 ◯ Numbers 30,31; Mark 9
3 ◯ Numbers 32,33; Mark 10
4 ◯ Numbers 34-36; Mark 11
5 ◯ Deut. 1,2; Mark 12
6 ◯ Deut.3,4; Ps. 36; Mark 13
7 ◯ Deut. 5,6; Ps. 43; Mark 14
8 ◯ Deut. 7-9; Mark 15
9 ◯ Deut. 10-12; Mark 16
10 ◯ Deut. 13-15; Galatians 1
11 ◯ Deut. 16-18; Ps. 38; Gal. 2
12 ◯ Deut. 19-21; Galatians 3
13 ◯ Deut. 22-24; Galatians 4
14 ◯ Deut. 25-27; Galatians 5
15 ◯ Deut. 28,29; Galatians 6
16 ◯ Deut. 30,31; Ps. 40; 1 Cor. 1
17 ◯ Deut. 32-34; 1 Cor. 2
18 ◯ Joshua 1,2; Ps. 37; 1 Cor. 3
19 ◯ Joshua 3-6; 1 Cor. 4
20 ◯ Joshua 7,8; Ps. 69; 1 Cor. 5
21 ◯ Joshua 9-11; 1 Cor. 6

22 ◯ Joshua 12-14; 1 Cor. 7
23 ◯ Joshua 15-17; 1 Cor. 8
24 ◯ Joshua 18-20; 1 Cor. 9
25 ◯ Joshua 21,22; Ps. 47; 1 Cor. 10
26 ◯ Joshua 23,24; Ps. 44; 1 Cor. 11
27 ◯ Judges 1-3; 1 Cor. 12
28 ◯ Judges 4,5; Ps. 39, 41; 1 Cor. 13
29 ◯ Judges 6,7; Ps. 52; & 1 Cor. 14
30 ◯ Judges 8; Ps. 42; 1 Cor. 15
31 ◯ Judges 9,10; Ps. 49; 1 Cor. 16

April

1 ◯ Judges 11,12; Ps. 50; 2 Cor. 1
2 ◯ Judges 13-16; 2 Cor. 2
3 ◯ Judges 17,18; Ps. 89; 2 Cor. 3
4 ◯ Judges 19-21; 2 Cor. 4
5 ◯ Ruth 1,2; Ps. 53, 61; 2 Cor. 5
6 ◯ Ruth 3,4; Ps. 64,65; 2 Cor. 6
7 ◯ 1 Samuel 1,2; Ps. 66; 2 Cor. 7
8 ◯ 1 Samuel 3-5; Ps. 77; 2 Cor. 8
9 ◯ 1 Samuel 6,7; Ps. 72; 2 Cor. 9
10 ◯ 1 Samuel 8-10; 2 Cor. 10
11 ◯ 1 Sam. 11,12; 1 Chr. 1; 2 Cor. 11
12 ◯ 1 Sam. 13; 1 Chr. 2,3; 2 Cor. 12
13 ◯ 1 Sam. 14; 1 Chr. 4; 2 Cor. 13
14 ◯ 1 Sam. 15,16; 1 Chr. 5; Mt. 1
15 ◯ 1 Sam. 17; Ps. 9; Mt. 2
16 ◯ 1 Sam. 18; 1 Chr. 6; Ps. 11; Mt. 3
17 ◯ 1 Sam. 19; 1 Chr. 7; Ps. 59; Mt. 4
18 ◯ 1 Sam. 20,21; Ps. 34; Mt. 5
19 ◯ 1 Sam. 22; Ps. 17,35; Mt. 6
20 ◯ 1 Sam. 23; Ps. 31,54; Mt. 7
21 ◯ 1 Sam. 24; Ps. 57,58; 1 Chr. 8; Mt 8
22 ◯ 1 Sam. 25,26; Ps. 63; Mt. 9
23 ◯ 1 Sam. 27; Ps. 141; 1 Chr. 9; Mt. 10
24 ◯ 1 Sam. 28,29; Ps. 109; Mt. 11
25 ◯ 1 Sam. 30,31; 1 Chr. 10; Mt. 12
26 ◯ 2 Sam. 1; Ps. 140; Mt. 13
27 ◯ 2 Sam. 2; 1 Chr. 11; Ps. 142; Mt. 14
28 ◯ 2 Sam. 3; 1 Chr. 12; Mt.15
29 ◯ 2 Sam. 4,5; Ps. 139; Mt. 16
30 ◯ 2 Sam. 6; 1 Chr. 13; Ps. 68; Mt. 17

May

1 ◯ 1 Chr. 14, 15; Ps. 132; Mt. 18
2 ◯ 1 Chr. 16; Ps. 106; Mt. 19
3 ◯ 2 Sam. 7; 1 Chr. 17; Ps. 2; Mt. 20
4 ◯ 2 Sam. 8, 9; 1 Chr. 18,19; Mt. 21
5 ◯ 2 Sam. 10; 1 Chr. 20; Ps. 20; Mt. 22
6 ◯ 2 Sam. 11,12; Ps. 51; Mt. 23

7 ◯ 2 Sam. 13, 14; Mt. 24
8 ◯ 2 Sam. 15,16; Ps. 32; Mt. 25
9 ◯ 2 Sam. 17; Ps. 71; Mt. 26
10 ◯ 2 Sam. 18; Ps. 56; Mt. 27
11 ◯ 2 Sam. 19,20; Ps. 55; Mt. 28
12 ◯ 2 Sam. 21-23; 1 Th. 1
13 ◯ 2 Sm. 24; 1 Chr. 21; Ps. 30; 1 Th. 2
14 ◯ 1 Chr. 22-24; 1 Th. 3
15 ◯ 1 Chr. 25-27; 1 Th. 4
16 ◯ 1 Ki. 1; 1 Chr. 28; Ps. 91; 1 Th. 5
17 ◯ 1 Ki. 2; 1 Chr. 29; Ps. 95; 2 Th. 1
18 ◯ 1 Ki. 3; 2 Chr. 1; Ps. 78; 2 Th. 2
19 ◯ 1 K. 4,5; 2 Chr. 2; Ps. 101; 2 Th. 3
20 ◯ 1 Ki. 6; 2 Chr. 3; Ps. 97; Rom. 1
21 ◯ 1 Ki. 7; 2 Chr. 4; Ps. 98; Rom. 2
22 ◯ 1 Ki. 8; 2 Chr. 5; Ps. 99; Rom. 3
23 ◯ 2 Chr. 6,7; Ps. 135; Rom. 4
24 ◯ 1 Ki. 9; 2 Chr. 8; Ps. 136; Rom. 5
25 ◯ 1 Ki. 10,11; 2 Chr. 9; Rom. 6
26 ◯ Prov. 1-3; Rom. 7
27 ◯ Prov. 4-6; Rom. 8
28 ◯ Prov. 7-9; Rom. 9
29 ◯ Prov. 10-12; Rom. 10
30 ◯ Prov. 13-15; Rom. 11
31 ◯ Prov. 16-18; Rom. 12

June

1 ◯ Prov. 19-21; Rom. 13
2 ◯ Prov. 22-24; Rom. 14
3 ◯ Prov 25-27; Rom. 15
4 ◯ Prov. 28-29; Ps. 60; Rom. 16
5 ◯ Prov. 30,31; Ps. 33; Eph. 1
6 ◯ Ecc. 1-3; Ps. 45; Eph. 2
7 ◯ Ecc. 4-6; Ps. 18; Eph. 3
8 ◯ Ecc. 7-9; Eph. 4
9 ◯ Ecc. 10-12; Ps. 94; Eph. 5
10 ◯ Song 1-4; Eph. 6
11 ◯ Song 5-8; Phil. 1
12 ◯ 1 Kings 12; 2 Chr. 10,11; Phil. 2
13 ◯ 1 Kings 13,14; 2 Chr. 12; Phil. 3
14 ◯ 1 Kings 15; 2 Chr. 13,14; Phil. 4
15 ◯ 1 Kings 16; 2 Chr. 15,16; Col. 1
16 ◯ 1 Kings 17-19; Col. 2
17 ◯ 1 Kings 20,21; 2 Chr. 17; Col. 3
18 ◯ 1 Kings 22; 2 Chr. 18,19; Col. 4
19 ◯ 2 Kings 1-3; Ps. 82; 1 Tim. 1
20 ◯ 2 Kings 4-5; Ps. 83; 1 Tim. 2
21 ◯ 2 Kings 6,7; 2 Chr. 20; 1 Tim. 3
22 ◯ 2 Kings 8,9; 2 Chr. 21; 1 Tim. 4
23 ◯ 2 Kings 10; 2 Chr. 22,23; 1 Tim. 5
24 ◯ 2 Kings 11,12; 2 Chr. 24; 1 Tim. 6

25 ◯ Joel 1-3; 2 Tim. 1
26 ◯ Jonah 1-4; 2 Tim. 2
27 ◯ 2 Kings 13,14; 2 Chr. 25; 2 Tim. 3
28 ◯ Amos 1-3; Ps. 80; 2 Tim. 4
29 ◯ Amos 4-6; Ps. 86, 87; Titus 1
30 ◯ Amos 7-9; Ps. 104; Titus 2

July

1 ◯ Is. 1-3; Titus 3
2 ◯ Is. 4,5; Ps. 115, 116; Jude
3 ◯ Is. 6,7; 2 Chr. 26,27; Philem.
4 ◯ 2 Ki. 15,16; Hos.1; Heb. 1
5 ◯ Hos. 2-5; Heb. 2
6 ◯ Hos. 6-9; Heb. 3
7 ◯ Hos. 10-12; Ps. 73; Heb. 4
8 ◯ Hos. 13,14; Ps. 100,102; Heb.5
9 ◯ Mic. 1-4; Heb. 6
10 ◯ Mic. 5-7; Heb. 7
11 ◯ Is. 8-10; Heb. 8
12 ◯ Is. 11-14; Heb. 9
13 ◯ Is. 15-18; Heb. 10
14 ◯ Is. 19-21; Heb. 11
15 ◯ Is. 22-24; Heb. 12
16 ◯ Is. 25-28; Heb. 13
17 ◯ Is. 29-31; James 1
18 ◯ Is. 32-35; James 2
19 ◯ 2 Ki. 17; 2 Chr. 28; Ps. 46; Jam.3
20 ◯ 2 Chr. 29-31; James 4
21 ◯ 2 Ki. 18,19; 2 Chr. 32; James 5
22 ◯ Is. 36,37; Ps. 76; 1 Pet. 1
23 ◯ 2 Ki. 20; Is. 38,39; Ps. 75; 1 Pet. 2
24 ◯ Is. 40-42; 1 Pet. 3
25 ◯ Is. 43-45; 1 Pet. 4
26 ◯ Is. 46-49; 1 Pet. 5
27 ◯ Is. 50-52; Ps. 92; 2 Pet. 1
28 ◯ Is. 53-56; 2 Pet.2
29 ◯ Is. 57-59; Ps. 103; 2 Pet. 3
30 ◯ Is. 60-62; Jn. 1
31 ◯ Is. 63,64; Ps. 107; Jn. 2

August

1 ◯ Is. 65,66; Ps. 62; Jn. 3
2 ◯ 2 Ki. 21; 2 Chr. 33; Jn. 4
3 ◯ Nah. 1-3; Jn. 5
4 ◯ 2 Ki. 22; 2 Chr. 34; Jn. 6
5 ◯ 2 Ki. 23; 2 Chr. 35; Jn. 7
6 ◯ Hab. 1-3; Jn. 8
7 ◯ Zeph. 1-3; Jn. 9
8 ◯ Jer. 1,2; Jn. 10
9 ◯ Jer. 3,4; Jn. 11

10 ◯ Jer. 5,6; Jn. 12
11 ◯ Jer. 7-9; Jn. 13
12 ◯ Jer. 10-12; Jn. 14
13 ◯ Jer. 13-15; Jn. 15
14 ◯ Jer. 16,17; Ps. 96; Jn. 16
15 ◯ Jer. 18-20; Ps. 93; Jn. 17
16 ◯ 2 Ki. 24; Jer. 22; Ps. 122; Jn. 18
17 ◯ Jer. 23,25; Jn. 19
18 ◯ Jer. 26,35,36; Jn. 20
19 ◯ Jer. 45-47; Ps. 105; Jn. 21
20 ◯ Jer. 48,49; Ps. 67; 1 Jn. 1
21 ◯ Jer. 21,24.27; Ps. 118; 1 Jn. 2
22 ◯ Jer. 28-30; 1 Jn. 3
23 ◯ Jer. 31,32; 1 Jn. 4
24 ◯ Jer. 33,34; Ps. 74; 1 Jn. 5
25 ◯ Jer. 37-39; Ps. 79; 2 Jn.
26 ◯ Jer. 50,51; 3 Jn.
27 ◯ Jer. 52; Rev. 1; Ps. 143,144
28 ◯ Ezek. 1-3; Rev. 2
29 ◯ Ezek. 4-7; Rev. 3
30 ◯ Ezek. 8-11; Rev. 4
31 ◯ Ezek. 12-14; Rev. 5

September

1 ◯ Ezek. 15,16; Ps. 70; Rev. 6
2 ◯ Ezek. 17-19; Rev. 7
3 ◯ Ezek. 20,21; Ps. 111; Rev. 8
4 ◯ Ezek. 22-24; Rev. 9
5 ◯ Ezek. 25-28; Rev. 10
6 ◯ Ezek. 29-32; Rev. 11
7 ◯ 2 Ki. 25; 2Chr. 36; Jer.40,41; Rev. 12
8 ◯ Jer. 42-44; Ps. 48; Rev. 13
9 ◯ Lam. 1,2; Obad; Rev. 14
10 ◯ Lam. 3-5; Rev. 15
11 ◯ Dan. 1,2; Rev. 16
12 ◯ Dan. 3,4; Ps. 81; Rev. 17
13 ◯ Ezek. 33-35; Rev. 18
14 ◯ Ezek. 36,37; Ps. 110; Rev. 19
15 ◯ Ezek. 38,39; Ps. 145; Rev. 20
16 ◯ Ezek. 40,41; Ps. 128; Rev. 21
17 ◯ Ezek. 42-44; Rev. 22
18 ◯ Ezek. 45,46; Lk. 1
19 ◯ Ezek. 47,48; Lk. 2
20 ◯ Dan. 5,6; Ps. 130; Lk. 3
21 ◯ Dan. 7,8; Ps. 137; Lk. 4
22 ◯ Dan. 9,10; Ps. 123; Lk. 5
23 ◯ Dan. 11,12; Lk. 6
24 ◯ Ezra 1; Ps. 84,85; Lk. 7
25 ◯ Ezra 2,3; Lk. 8
26 ◯ Ezra 4; Ps. 113,127; Lk. 9
27 ◯ Hag. 1,2; Ps. 129; Lk. 10
28 ◯ Zech. 1-3; Lk. 11

29 ◯ Zech. 4-6; Lk. 12
30 ◯ Zech. 7-9; Lk. 13

October

1 ◯ Zech. 10-12; Ps. 126; Lk. 14
2 ◯ Zech. 13,14; Ps. 147; Lk. 15
3 ◯ Ezra 5,6; Ps. 138; Lk. 16
4 ◯ Est. 1,2; Ps. 150; Lk. 17
5 ◯ Est. 3-8; Lk. 18
6 ◯ Est. 9,10; Lk. 19
7 ◯ Ezra 7,8; Lk. 20
8 ◯ Ezra 9, 10; Ps. 131; Lk. 21
9 ◯ Neh. 1,2; Ps. 133, 134; Lk. 22
10 ◯ Neh. 3,4; Lk. 23
11 ◯ Neh. 5,6; Ps. 146; Lk. 24
12 ◯ Neh. 7,8; Acts 1
13 ◯ Neh. 9, 10; Acts 2
14 ◯ Neh. 11,12; Ps. 1; Acts 3
15 ◯ Neh. 13; Mal. 1,2; Acts 4
16 ◯ Mal. 3,4; Ps. 148; Acts 5
17 ◯ Job 1,2; Acts 6,7
18 ◯ Job 3,4; Acts 8,9
19 ◯ Job 5; Ps. 108; Acts 10, 11
20 ◯ Job 6-8; Acts 12
21 ◯ Job 9, 10; Acts 13,14
22 ◯ Job 11,12; Acts 15,16
23 ◯ Job 13,14; Acts 17,18
24 ◯ Job 15; Acts 19, 20
25 ◯ Job 16; Acts 21-23
26 ◯ Job 17; Acts 24-26
27 ◯ Job 18; Ps. 114; Acts 27,28
28 ◯ Job 19; Mk. 1,2
29 ◯ Job 20; Mk. 3,4
30 ◯ Job 21; Mk. 5,6
31 ◯ Job 22; Mk. 7,8

November

1 ◯ Ps. 121; Mk. 9, 10
2 ◯ Job 23, 24; Mk. 11,12
3 ◯ Job 25; Mk. 13,14
4 ◯ Job 26,27; Mk. 15,16
5 ◯ Job 28,29; Gal. 1,2
6 ◯ Job 30; Ps. 120; Gal. 3,4
7 ◯ Job 31,32; Gal. 5,6
8 ◯ Job 33; 1 Cor. 1-3
9 ◯ Job 34; 1 Cor. 4-6
10 ◯ Job 35,36; 1 Cor. 7,8
11 ◯ Ps. 122; 1 Cor. 9-11
12 ◯ Job 37,38; 1 Cor. 12
13 ◯ Job 39,40; 1 Cor. 13,14

14 ◯ Ps. 149; 1 Cor. 15,16
15 ◯ Job 41,42; 2 Cor. 1,2
16 ◯ 2 Cor. 3-6
17 ◯ 2 Cor. 7-10
18 ◯ Ps. 124; 2 Cor. 11-13
19 ◯ Mt. 1-4
20 ◯ Mt. 5-7
21 ◯ Mt. 8-10
22 ◯ Mt. 11-13
23 ◯ Mt. 14-16
24 ◯ Mt. 17-19
25 ◯ Mt. 20-22
26 ◯ Mt. 23-25
27 ◯ Ps. 125; Mt. 26,27
28 ◯ Mt. 28; 1 Th. 1-3
29 ◯ 1 Th. 4,5; 2 Th. 1-3
30 ◯ Rom. 1-4

December

1 ◯ Rom. 5-8
2 ◯ Rom. 9-12
3 ◯ Rom. 13-16
4 ◯ Eph. 1-4
5 ◯ Eph. 5,6; Ps. 119: 1-80
6 ◯ Phil. 1-4
7 ◯ Col. 1-4
8 ◯ 1 Tim. 1-4
9 ◯ 1 Tim. 5,6; Titus 1-3
10 ◯ 2 Tim. 1-4
11 ◯ Philem.; Heb. 1-4
12 ◯ Heb. 5-8
13 ◯ Heb. 9-11
14 ◯ Heb. 12,13; Jude
15 ◯ Jas. 1-5
16 ◯ 1 Pet. 1-5
17 ◯ 2 Pet. 1-3; Jn. 1
18 ◯ Jn. 2-4
19 ◯ Jn. 5,6
20 ◯ Jn. 7,8
21 ◯ Jn. 9-11
22 ◯ Jn. 12-14
23 ◯ Jn. 15-18
24 ◯ Jn. 19-21
25 ◯ 1 Jn. 1-5
26 ◯ Ps. 117,119: 81-176; 2 Jn.; 3 Jn.
27 ◯ Rev. 1-4
28 ◯ Rev. 5-9
29 ◯ Rev. 10-14
30 ◯ Rev. 15-18
31 ◯ Rev. 19-22

Date   _Title_

S _____

O _____

A _____

P _____

Date   *Title*

S

O

A

P

Date   *Title*

S _____

O _____

A _____

P _____

Date　　　　　　　*Title*

_____

_____

S_____

_____

_____

_____

O_____

_____

_____

_____

_____

A_____

_____

_____

_____

_____

P_____

_____

_____

_____

Date

Title

S _____

O _____

A _____

P _____

JesusFreakApparel.com

Date   *Title*

S

O

A

P

Date   *Title*

S

O

A

P

Date   Title

_____

S_____

_____

_____

_____

_____

O_____

_____

_____

_____

_____

A_____

_____

_____

_____

_____

P_____

_____

_____

_____

Date   *Title*

_____

S_____

_____

_____

_____

O_____

_____

_____

_____

A_____

_____

_____

_____

P_____

_____

_____

_____

Date　　　　　　　*Title*

_____

_____

*S*_____

_____

_____

_____

_____

*O*_____

_____

_____

_____

_____

_____

*A*_____

_____

_____

_____

_____

_____

*P*_____

_____

_____

_____

_____

Date   *Title*

_____

S_____

_____

_____

_____

O_____

_____

_____

_____

_____

A_____

_____

_____

_____

_____

P_____

_____

_____

_____

Date   *Title*

_____

S_____

_____

_____

_____

O_____

_____

_____

_____

A_____

_____

_____

_____

P_____

_____

_____

_____

Date   *Title*

_____

*S*_____

_____

_____

_____

_____

*O*_____

_____

_____

_____

_____

*A*_____

_____

_____

_____

_____

*P*_____

_____

_____

_____

_____

Date   *Title*

S

O

A

P

Date   *Title*

S

O

A

P

Date   *Title*

_____

S_____

_____

_____

_____

O_____

_____

_____

_____

_____

𝒜_____

_____

_____

_____

_____

𝒫_____

_____

_____

_____

Date   *Title*

S_____

_____

_____

O_____

_____

_____

_____

A_____

_____

_____

_____

P_____

_____

_____

_____

Date   Title

S _____

O _____

A _____

P _____

Date   *Title*

_____

S_____

_____

_____

_____

O_____

_____

_____

_____

A_____

_____

_____

_____

P_____

_____

_____

_____

_____

Date   Title

_____

S _____

_____

_____

_____

O _____

_____

_____

_____

A _____

_____

_____

_____

P _____

_____

_____

_____

Date _____   Title _____

_____

S_____

_____

_____

_____

O_____

_____

_____

_____

A_____

_____

_____

_____

P_____

_____

_____

_____

Date   *Title*

S

O

A

P

Date   *Title*

_____

S _____

_____

_____

_____

O _____

_____

_____

_____

A _____

_____

_____

_____

P _____

_____

_____

_____

Date

Title

S _____

O _____

A _____

P _____

Date *Title*

S

O

$\mathcal{A}$

P

JESUS FREAK
JesusFreakApparel.com

Date   *Title*

S

O

A

P

Date   Title

S

O

A

P

Date　　　　　　　*Title*

_____

S_____

_____

_____

_____

O_____

_____

_____

_____

A_____

_____

_____

_____

P_____

_____

_____

_____

Date   *Title*

_____

S _____

_____

_____

_____

O _____

_____

_____

_____

_____

$\mathcal{A}$ _____

_____

_____

_____

_____

$\mathcal{P}$ _____

_____

_____

_____

JesusFreakApparel.com

Date   Title

_____

S_____

_____

_____

O_____

_____

_____

_____

A_____

_____

_____

_____

P_____

_____

_____

_____

Date   *Title*

S_____

O_____

A_____

P_____

Date   *Title*

_____

S _____

_____

_____

_____

O _____

_____

_____

_____

_____

A _____

_____

_____

_____

_____

P _____

_____

_____

_____

Date   *Title*

_____

S_____

_____

_____

_____

O_____

_____

_____

_____

_____

A_____

_____

_____

_____

_____

P_____

_____

_____

_____

Date *Title*

S_____

O_____

A_____

P_____

Date   Title

S _____

O _____

A _____

P _____

Date   *Title*

S

O

A

P

Date   *Title*

_____

*S*_____

_____

_____

_____

*O*_____

_____

_____

_____

_____

*A*_____

_____

_____

_____

_____

*P*_____

_____

_____

_____

Date *Title*

S_____

_____

O_____

_____

_____

A_____

_____

_____

P_____

_____

Date   *Title*

_____

S_____

_____

_____

O_____

_____

_____

_____

𝒜_____

_____

_____

_____

𝒫_____

_____

_____

_____

Date   Title

S

O

A

P

Date *Title*

S_____

O_____

A_____

P_____

Date   Title

S _____

O _____

A _____

P _____

Date   Title

_____

_____
S _____

_____

_____

_____

O _____

_____

_____

_____

_____

A _____

_____

_____

_____

P _____

_____

_____

_____

Date   _Title_

S_____

_____

O_____

_____

A_____

_____

P_____

_____

Date　　　　　　*Title*

S_____

O_____

A_____

P_____

JesusFreakApparel.com

Date   *Title*

S

O

A

P

Date　　　　　　*Title*

S

O

A

P

Date   *Title*

S _____

O _____

A _____

P _____

Date   *Title*

S_____

O_____

A_____

P_____

Date   *Title*

S _____

O _____

A _____

P _____

Date *Title*

S

O

A

P

Date   *Title*

S

O

A

P

Date _____ Title _____

S _____

O _____

A _____

P _____

JESUS FREAK
JesusFreakApparel.com

Date   *Title*

S _____

_____

O _____

_____

A _____

_____

P _____

_____

Date   *Title*

S

O

A

P

Date   *Title*

_____

S_____

_____

_____

_____

O_____

_____

_____

_____

_____

A_____

_____

_____

_____

_____

P_____

_____

_____

_____

Date   *Title*

S

O

A

P

Date *Title*

S

O

A

P

Date   *Title*

_____

S_____

_____

_____

_____

O_____

_____

_____

_____

_____

A_____

_____

_____

_____

_____

P_____

_____

_____

_____

Date

Title

S

O

A

P

Date　　　　　　　*Title*

S _____

O _____

A _____

P _____

Date   Title

S

O

A

P

Date   Title

S _____

O _____

𝒜 _____

𝒫 _____

Date   *Title*

S

O

A

P

Date   *Title*

_____

S_____

_____

_____

_____

O_____

_____

_____

_____

𝒜_____

_____

_____

_____

𝒫_____

_____

_____

_____

Date _____   Title _____

_____

S _____

_____

_____

_____

O _____

_____

_____

_____

A _____

_____

_____

_____

P _____

_____

_____

_____

Date   *Title*

S_____

O_____

A_____

P_____

Date   Title

S

O

A

P

Date   *Title*

S

O

A

P

JESUS FREAK

JesusFreakApparel.com

Date   *Title*

S_____

O_____

A_____

P_____

Date   *Title*

S_____

_____

_____

_____

O_____

_____

_____

_____

A_____

_____

_____

_____

P_____

_____

_____

_____

Date   Title

S_____

O_____

A_____

P_____

Date   *Title*

*S*_____

*O*_____

*A*_____

*P*_____

Date　　　　　　　　*Title*

S

O

A

P

Date   *Title*

S

O

A

P

Date   *Title*

_____

S_____

_____

_____

_____

O_____

_____

_____

_____

_____

A_____

_____

_____

_____

_____

P_____

_____

_____

_____

Date   *Title*

_____

S_____

_____

_____

_____

O_____

_____

_____

_____

_____

A_____

_____

_____

_____

_____

P_____

_____

_____

_____

Date   *Title*

S_____

O_____

A_____

P_____

Date   *Title*

_____

S_____

_____

_____

_____

O_____

_____

_____

_____

A_____

_____

_____

_____

P_____

_____

_____

_____

Date   *Title*

S_____

O_____

A_____

P_____

Date   *Title*

S_____

O_____

A_____

P_____

Date   *Title*

S _____

O _____

A _____

P _____

Date   Title

S

O

A

P

Date   Title

_____

S_____

_____

_____

_____

O_____

_____

_____

_____

_____

A_____

_____

_____

_____

P_____

_____

_____

_____

Date _____ Title _____

_____

S _____

_____

_____

_____

O _____

_____

_____

_____

A _____

_____

_____

_____

P _____

_____

_____

_____

Date   *Title*

S

O

A

P

Date   Title

_____

S_____

_____

_____

_____

O_____

_____

_____

_____

A_____

_____

_____

_____

P_____

_____

_____

_____

Date   *Title*

_____

S_____

_____

_____

_____

O_____

_____

_____

_____

A_____

_____

_____

_____

P_____

_____

_____

_____

Date   *Title*

S _____

O _____

A _____

P _____

Date　　　　　　　*Title*

S_____

O_____

A_____

P_____

Date   *Title*

_____

S_____

_____

_____

_____

O_____

_____

_____

_____

A_____

_____

_____

_____

P_____

_____

_____

_____

Date _____ Title _____

_____

_____

S _____

_____

_____

_____

O _____

_____

_____

_____

_____

A _____

_____

_____

_____

_____

P _____

_____

_____

_____

_____

Date   *Title*

S

O

A

P

Date   *Title*

S_____

O_____

A_____

P_____

Date   *Title*

_____

_____

S_____

_____

_____

_____

O_____

_____

_____

_____

A_____

_____

_____

_____

P_____

_____

_____

_____

Date　　　　　*Title*

_____

S_____

_____

_____

_____

O_____

_____

_____

_____

A_____

_____

_____

_____

P_____

_____

_____

_____

Date   *Title*

S _____

O _____

A _____

P _____

Date   *Title*

S

O

A

P

Date   Title

_____

S_____

_____

_____

_____

O_____

_____

_____

_____

_____

A_____

_____

_____

_____

_____

P_____

_____

_____

_____

Date   Title

_____

S_____

_____

_____

_____

O_____

_____

_____

_____

_____

A_____

_____

_____

_____

_____

P_____

_____

_____

_____

Date　　　　　　*Title*

S _____

_____

O _____

_____

A _____

_____

P _____

_____

Date   *Title*

S

O

A

P

Date *Title*

S

O

A

P

Date   Title

_____

S_____

_____

_____

O_____

_____

_____

_____

A_____

_____

_____

_____

P_____

_____

_____

_____

Date   *Title*

_____

S_____

_____

_____

_____

_____

O_____

_____

_____

_____

_____

A_____

_____

_____

_____

_____

P_____

_____

_____

_____

Date   *Title*

S_____

O_____

A_____

P_____

Date   *Title*

S _____

O _____

A _____

P _____

Date   *Title*

_____
_____
S_____
_____
_____
_____
_____
O_____
_____
_____
_____
_____
A_____
_____
_____
_____
_____
P_____
_____
_____
_____
_____

Date *Title*

S_____

O_____

A_____

P_____

Date *Title*

S_____

_____

O_____

_____

𝒜_____

_____

𝒫_____

_____

Date   *Title*

S

O

A

P

Date   Title

_S_ _____

_____

_____

_____

_O_ _____

_____

_____

_____

_____

_A_ _____

_____

_____

_____

_____

_P_ _____

_____

_____

_____

Date   *Title*

S _____

O _____

A _____

P _____

Date _____ Title _____

_____

S_____

_____

_____

_____

O_____

_____

_____

_____

A_____

_____

_____

_____

P_____

_____

_____

_____

Date   *Title*

S

O

A

P

Date   *Title*

_____

*S*_____

_____

_____

_____

*O*_____

_____

_____

_____

_____

*A*_____

_____

_____

_____

_____

*P*_____

_____

_____

_____

Date _____   Title _____

_____

S_____

_____

_____

_____

O_____

_____

_____

_____

A_____

_____

_____

_____

P_____

_____

_____

_____

Date *Title*

S

O

A

P

Date _____   Title _____

_____

S_____

_____

_____

_____

O_____

_____

_____

_____

A_____

_____

_____

_____

P_____

_____

_____

_____

Date   Title

_____

S_____

_____

_____

_____

O_____

_____

_____

_____

A_____

_____

_____

_____

P_____

_____

_____

_____

Date　　　　　*Title*

S _____

O _____

A _____

P _____

JesusFreakApparel.com

Date   *Title*

S

O

A

P

Date   *Title*

S

O

A

P

Date _____   *Title* _____

_____

S _____

_____

_____

_____

O _____

_____

_____

_____

_____

A _____

_____

_____

_____

_____

P _____

_____

_____

_____

Date   *Title*

S

O

A

P

Date   Title

_____

_____

S_____

_____

_____

_____

_____

O_____

_____

_____

_____

_____

A_____

_____

_____

_____

_____

P_____

_____

_____

_____

Date　　　　　　　*Title*

S

O

A

P

Date   *Title*

S_____

O_____

𝒜_____

𝒫_____

Date *Title*

S_____

O_____

A_____

P_____

Date   *Title*

S_____

O_____

A_____

P_____

Date　　　　　　　*Title*

S

O

A

P

Date   Title

_____

S_____

_____

_____

O_____

_____

_____

_____

A_____

_____

_____

_____

P_____

_____

_____

_____

Date   *Title*

_____

S _____

_____

_____

_____

O _____

_____

_____

_____

A _____

_____

_____

_____

P _____

_____

_____

_____

Date   Title

S

O

A

P

Date   *Title*

S _____

O _____

A _____

P _____

Date   *Title*

_____

S_____

_____

_____

_____

O_____

_____

_____

_____

A_____

_____

_____

_____

P_____

_____

_____

_____

Date   *Title*

_____

S_____

_____

_____

_____

O_____

_____

_____

_____

A_____

_____

_____

_____

P_____

_____

_____

_____

JesusFreakApparel.com

Date   *Title*

_____

_____

S_____

_____

_____

_____

O_____

_____

_____

_____

_____

A_____

_____

_____

_____

_____

P_____

_____

_____

_____

Date   *Title*

*S*_____

_____

*O*_____

_____

*A*_____

_____

*P*_____

_____

Date   Title

_____

S_____

_____

_____

_____

O_____

_____

_____

_____

A_____

_____

_____

_____

P_____

_____

_____

_____

Date   *Title*

S

O

A

P

Date   Title

_____

S_____

_____

_____

O_____

_____

_____

_____

A_____

_____

_____

_____

P_____

_____

_____

_____

Date   *Title*

S_____

_____

_____

_____

O_____

_____

_____

_____

𝒜_____

_____

_____

_____

𝒫_____

_____

_____

_____

Date   *Title*

S _____

O _____

A _____

P _____

Date *Title*

S_____

O_____

$\mathcal{A}$_____

$\mathcal{P}$_____

JesusFreakApparel.com

Date   *Title*

S

O

A

P

Date   *Title*

S_____

O_____

A_____

P_____

RECOVERING SINNER
ADOPTED BY CHRIST
SAVED BY GRACE

JESUSFREAKAPPAREL.COM

Date   Title

_____

*S*_____

_____

_____

_____

_____

*O*_____

_____

_____

_____

_____

*A*_____

_____

_____

_____

_____

*P*_____

_____

_____

_____

Date   *Title*

S _____

O _____

A _____

P _____

Date   *Title*

S_____

O_____

A_____

P_____

Date   *Title*

S

O

A

P

Date

Title

S

O

A

P

Date

Title

S

O

A

P

JesusFreakApparel.com

Date   *Title*

S

O

A

P

Date   *Title*

S _____

O _____

A _____

P _____

RECOVERING SINNER
ADOPTED BY CHRIST
SAVED BY GRACE

Date   *Title*

_____

*S*_____

_____

_____

_____

*O*_____

_____

_____

_____

*A*_____

_____

_____

_____

*P*_____

_____

_____

_____

Date　　　　　*Title*

S_____

_____

_____

O_____

_____

_____

_____

A_____

_____

_____

_____

P_____

_____

_____

JesusFreakApparel.com

Date　　　　　　　*Title*

S _____

O _____

A _____

P _____

Date   *Title*

_____

S_____

_____

_____

O_____

_____

_____

_____

A_____

_____

_____

_____

P_____

_____

_____

Date _____ **Title** _____

_____

_____

S _____

_____

_____

_____

_____

O _____

_____

_____

_____

_____

A _____

_____

_____

_____

_____

P _____

_____

_____

_____

Date   *Title*

S _____

O _____

A _____

P _____

Date   Title

S _____

_____

O _____

_____

A _____

_____

P _____

_____

Date   *Title*

S

O

$\mathcal{A}$

$\mathcal{P}$

Date   *Title*

S _____

O _____

A _____

P _____

Date   *Title*

_____

S _____

_____

_____

_____

O _____

_____

_____

_____

A _____

_____

_____

_____

P _____

_____

_____

_____

Date　　　　　*Title*

S

O

A

P

Date   Title

S

O

A

P

Date   *Title*

_____

_____

S_____

_____

_____

_____

O_____

_____

_____

_____

A_____

_____

_____

_____

_____

P_____

_____

_____

_____

Date   Title

S

O

A

P

Date   *Title*

S_____

O_____

𝒜_____

𝒫_____

Date　　　　　*Title*

S _____

O _____

A _____

P _____

RECOVERING SINNER
ADOPTED BY CHRIST
SAVED BY GRACE

Date   Title

_____

S_____

_____

_____

_____

O_____

_____

_____

_____

A_____

_____

_____

_____

P_____

_____

_____

_____

Date　　　　*Title*

S _____

_____

_____

_____

O _____

_____

_____

_____

A _____

_____

_____

_____

P _____

_____

_____

_____

JesusFreakApparel.com

Date   *Title*

S _____

_____

O _____

_____

A _____

_____

P _____

_____

Date　　　　　　*Title*

S _____

O _____

A _____

P _____

Date   Title

_____

S_____

_____

_____

_____

O_____

_____

_____

_____

A_____

_____

_____

_____

_____

P_____

_____

_____

_____

Date

Title

S

O

A

P

JESUS FREAK

JesusFreakApparel.com

Date _____ Title _____

_____

S _____

_____

_____

_____

O _____

_____

_____

_____

A _____

_____

_____

_____

P _____

_____

_____

_____

Date　　　　　　　　*Title*

S

O

A

P

Date   Title

S _____

O _____

A _____

P _____

Date   *Title*

_____

S_____

_____

_____

_____

O_____

_____

_____

_____

A_____

_____

_____

_____

P_____

_____

_____

_____

About the Author

Sandy Holly is passionate about reading, studying, and proclaiming the Word of God, and that is why her company, *Jesus Freak Apparel,* is a proud supporter of Compassion International and Klove Christian radio. Compassion International releases children from poverty around the world in Jesus' name. Klove provides positive and encouraging stories from other Christians and inspiring music through Christian radio, which is broadcast around the world for all to hear about Jesus. To learn more about these organizations, please visit Sandy's online store at JesusFreakApparel.com and learn how your purchase promotes the Good News for all to hear.

"The grass withers and the flowers fade, but the word of our God stands forever." (Isaiah 40:8, NLT)

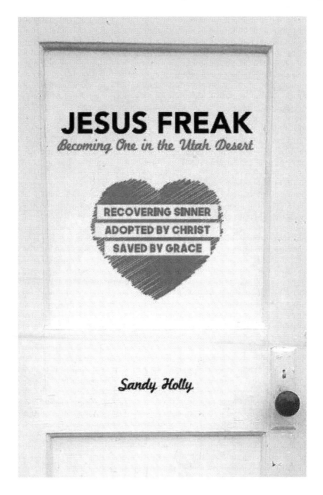

In 2008 God led me to the middle of the Utah desert and stripped me of everything I knew to be true and right. He took away the complacent, the lukewarm, and the getting by, and revealed Himself to me. He ignited a spark that started within me a blazing fire for Him, like only the Creator of the universe can. He put me back together, and when He did, He gifted me with parts of Him. He gave me greater patience, compassion, and love for others. And with these gifts, He stole my heart. And thank God, I have never been the same.

Yahoo! It's Time to Tell Your Story!
In your own Personal Journal available at JesusFreakApparel.com

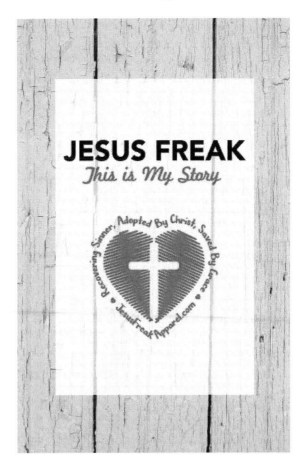

Everyone has a story to tell. May I encourage you to write your story and explore your life? Journaling your personal experience is a way of organizing your thoughts and helps you remember the character of God. You will find the places where God has shown up in the most beautiful ways. It was through journaling that God had the opportunity to grow and shape me. Will you let Him shape you?